# MY LITTLE GOLDEN BOOK OF
# Manners

By PEGGY PARISH

*Consultants: The Third Grade
at Dalton School, New York*

Illustrated by
RICHARD SCARRY

As we're sure you've all noticed, animals are very well behaved indeed—more so than many small girls and boys. Tail-wagging and paw-licking and kangaroo-hopping and lion-leaping are almost always done in a most ladylike or gentlemanly manner.

Because animals are so very, very polite, we thought we would ask some of our furry and feathered friends to show, in the pictures that illustrate this book, how good their manners really are.

The Editors

# A GOLDEN BOOK · NEW YORK

## Western Publishing Company, Inc., Racine, Wisconsin 53404

Good manners make a person nice to know.
Good manners mean being kind and helpful
   and friendly to people, all day, every day.
Here are some good manners to learn.
BEFORE YOU GO TO THE TABLE:
Wash your hands and face,
   and brush your hair.

AT THE TABLE:
Sit up nice and straight.
Keep your elbows off the table
   and keep your feet on the floor.
Don't wiggle or squirm or shout.
Put your napkin in your lap.

Silverware is NOT to play with.
Use your knife to cut your food.
Use your fork to pick up your food.
*Say "Please" when you ask for something.*
*Say "Thank you" when you are given something.*

Chew your food with your mouth closed.
Never try to talk with your mouth full.
AT THE END OF A MEAL:
Put your silverware on your plate.
Put your napkin beside your plate.
Say "May I be excused, please?" if you
   want to leave the table.

INVITING FRIENDS TO YOUR HOUSE MEANS
   seeing that your friends have a good time.
Greet each of your guests with a
   Hello and Please-come-in.
Show them where to put their hats and coats.

If you have a friend who doesn't know everyone,
   say "I would like you to meet my friend,"
   and say your friend's name.

Be sure to serve your friends
   food and drink
   before you serve yourself.

Help all your friends to join in the fun.
If a friend is shy,
  be especially kind,
  and help him make friends
  with the others.
Ask your friends what games
  they would like to play.

When your friends leave,
thank them for coming
to your party.

A boy should help a girl with her coat.
Hold the door open for a girl or a grown-up.
Let a girl or a grown-up go first.

GOING TO A PARTY AT A FRIEND'S HOUSE MEANS
helping him to see that everyone has a good time.
Say "Hello" to your friend and to his mother.
Say "Hello" to all his friends.
Be cheerful and friendly.

Don't touch things or play with things
until you ask if you may.
*Say "Please" if you want something.*
*Say "Thank you" if you are given something.*

When you leave, tell your friend and
your friend's mother that you had a nice time.
Say "Good-bye" and say "Thank you."

WHEN YOU TELEPHONE A FRIEND'S HOUSE,
   say who you are,
   and say "May I speak to my friend, please?"

When you answer the telephone in your house,
   say who you are.
Say "Please wait, I will call Mommy or Daddy."
Put the telephone down gently, so that it won't
   make a noise in the other person's ear.

If Mommy or Daddy is not at home,
say "May I take a message?"
Listen carefully to the message,
and tell Mommy or Daddy the message
when they come home.

IF YOU ARE GOING ON A BUS OR A TRAIN,
   wait for your turn to get on.
Don't push.
Say "Excuse me" if you want to pass.
Say "I'm sorry" if you bump into someone.

Don't stare and point at people.
It may hurt their feelings.
Don't put your feet on the seats.

On a bus or a train,
   don't sit down if grown-ups are standing.
If there is no seat for them,
   get up and say "Won't you please sit down?"

In a bus or a train, or in a restaurant,
don't talk loudly or shout.

Don't run around.

Cover your mouth
  when you cough
  or yawn
  or sneeze.

AAAhhh

A BOY SHOULD REMOVE HIS HAT
   when he meets a lady,
   in a church,
   when the flag goes by,
   in an elevator.

Good manners are not just things to learn.
Good manners help to make a person think
of other people,
and how to make them happy.
Good manners help to make a person nice
to know.